D1436227

Dangerous and Dastardly Animals

Interactive Quiz

Managing Editors: Simon Melhuish and Sarah Wells
Series Editor: Nikole G Bamford
Designer: Linley J Clode
Writer: CAS
Illustrator: Gary Sherwood
Additional Contributors: Paul Lucas

Published by
The Lagoon Group
PO Box 311, KT2 5QW, UK
PO Box 990676, Boston, MA 02199, USA

ISBN: 1904797083

www.thelagoongroup.com

Printed in China

Dangerous and Dastardly Animals

Interactive Quiz

IntelliQuest

UNIQUE BOOK CODE	006

Instructions

First of all make sure you have a Quizmo —

Find the book's unique code (this appears at the top of this page). Use the < and > buttons to scroll to this number on the Quizmo screen. Press the ⬥ button to enter the code, and you're ready to go.

Use the < > scroll buttons to select the question number you want to answer. Press the A, B, C, or D button to enter your chosen answer.

If you are correct the green light beside the button you pressed will flash. You can then use the scroll button to move on to another question.

If your answer is incorrect, the red light beside the button you pressed will flash.

Don't worry, you can try again and again until you have the correct answer, OR move on to another question. (Beware: the more times you guess incorrectly, the lower your final percentage score will be!)

You can finish the quiz at any point – just press the ⬅ button to find out your score and rank as follows:

75% or above	You sure are wild about wild animals!
50% – 74%	A GRRRRRRRREAT performance!
25% – 49%	Sharpen your claws - you're not up to scratch!
Less than 25%	You're at the bottom of the food chain...

If you do press the ⬅ button to find out your score, this will end your session and you will have to use the ⬅ to start again!

HAVE FUN!

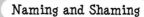

Naming and Shaming

001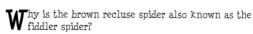

Why is the brown recluse spider also known as the fiddler spider?

- **A)** Because its body is shaped like a violin
- **B)** Because its web is shaped like a violin
- **C)** Because it has a spot on its back like a violin
- **D)** Because it makes a sound like a violin when frightened

002

What animal kills more people in Africa than any other?

- **A)** Lion
- **B)** Hippopotamus
- **C)** Rhinoceros
- **D)** Crocodile

003

Which animal produces the most toxic biological substance known?

- **A)** Vampire bat
- **B)** King cobra
- **C)** Poison-dart tree frog
- **D)** Black widow

004

What type of creature is a sea wasp?

- **A)** A jellyfish
- **B)** A dragonfly
- **C)** A seahorse
- **D)** A swordfish

Naming and Shaming

Which one of these is a deadly African snake?
- **A)** Bamba
- **B)** Ramba
- **C)** Mumba
- **D)** Mamba

005

Which one of these is a real-life dragon?
- **A)** Komodo dragon
- **B)** Asian red dragon
- **C)** African puff dragon
- **D)** Norwegian black dragon

006

Which shell-plated fiend has jaws strong enough to bite off your finger?
- **A)** Spring-jawed tortoise
- **B)** Venus fly trap
- **C)** Saber-toothed lobster
- **D)** Snapping turtle

007

The black widow is a lethal type of what?
- **A)** Scorpion
- **B)** Spider
- **C)** Housefly
- **D)** Fish

008

009

How did the aggressive funnel web spider get its name?

- **A)** From the shape of its web
- **B)** Because it weaves webs in ship funnels
- **C)** From the shape of its body
- **D)** The first one was discovered in a ship's funnel

010

Carpet beetles lay their eggs in carpets and eat the wool and dead insects in it. What are their larvae known as?

- **A)** Woolly mittens
- **B)** Woolly lambs
- **C)** Woolly jumpers
- **D)** Woolly bears

011

Which small animal's spine is so strong that it is said a man can't squash even if he stands on it?

- **A)** Water vole
- **B)** Rockback mouse
- **C)** Flat rat
- **D)** Hero shrew

012

Which of the following big cats has never attacked man?

- **A)** Cheetah
- **B)** Lion
- **C)** Tiger
- **D)** Leopard

Naming and Shaming

How did grizzly bears get their name?

013

A) They have long frosted hairs on their back and shoulders giving them a grizzled appearance

B) They kill their prey in a grizzly manner

C) They always appear grumpy

D) Their babies cry a lot in the first year

What is a fugu?

014

A) A Japanese snake

B) A type of venomous frog

C) A sea urchin

D) A pufferfish

Why is the cookie cutter shark so called?

015

A) Because its mouth is completely circular

B) Because it gouges a circle of flesh out of its prey

C) It has circular holes in its fins

D) Because it has circular markings on its body

Which animal can eat stonefish and be unaffected by its venom?

016

A) Humans

B) Large-headed seasnake

C) Gulper eels

D) Hammerhead shark

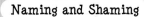

017

Which of the following can kill fish instantly with paralysing venom?

A) Piranha
B) Hatchet fish
C) Rat trap fish
D) Cone shells

018

Which animal carries the bubonic plague virus?

A) Mice
B) Rats
C) Fleas
D) Squirrels

019

Conenose bugs are bloodsucking parasites and are also known as what?

A) Killer bugs
B) Assassin bugs
C) Sniper bugs
D) Butcher bug

020

How did the deathwatch beetle get its name?

A) It only ever crawls on people who are about to die
B) Its sound used to be the only thing heard at night by people in their sick beds
C) It will stay beside an injured mate until it dies
D) It has markings like a skull on its back

Volcanic vents are both incredibly hot and full of toxic chemicals. Which of the following animals can survive the extreme environment?

A) Giant tubeworm

B) Fire beetle

C) Woodlouse

D) All of the above

Which single animal, according to the rhyme, denotes sorrow?

A) Jackdaw

B) Magpie

C) Crow

D) Rook

Which beetle has an internal combustion chamber and can spray lethal boiling acid?

A) Colorado beetle

B) Crippen squid

C) Commando lizard

D) Bombardier beetle

What is another name for the Portuguese man o'war?

A) Lionfish

B) Snapping turtle

C) Bluebottle jellyfish

D) Manatee

025

How did the Tasmanian Devil get its name?

- **A)** Because it has a forked tongue
- **B)** Because it has tiny horns
- **C)** Because of its cloven hooves
- **D)** Because of its eerie growl which progresses from whistle to bark

026

What is the correct term for a pregnant goldfish?

- **A)** A twit
- **B)** A loon
- **C)** A fool
- **D)** A berk

027

Which of these monsters is real?

- **A)** Gila monster
- **B)** Gorgon
- **C)** Chimera
- **D)** Titan

028

The Beast of Bodmin Moor and The Beast of Billericay were animals people claimed to have seen stalking the English countryside. What are they believed to be?

- **A)** Giant hounds
- **B)** Panthers
- **C)** Brown bears
- **D)** Wolves

Senses

What percentage of a shark's brain is dedicated to its sense of smell?

A) 25
B) 70
C) 60
D) 45

029

What smell excites a shark?

A) Flowers
B) Perfume
C) Blood
D) Salt

030

What animals, common in the USA, are attracted to electrical fields and live in electrical equipment in your homes, (e.g. televisions, computers, air-conditioning equipment)?

A) Houseflies
B) Fire ants
C) Caterpillars
D) Gremlins

031

What are wasps most aggravated by?

A) Light clothes and acrid odors
B) Dark clothes and sweet odors
C) Red clothes and fruity smells
D) White clothes and salty smells

032

033

Bluebottles can smell meat from how far away?

A) 0.6m/1km
B) 2.5m/4km
C) 4.3m/7km
D) 6.2/10km

034

Which of these has hearing so accurate they can sense movement of less than a millionth of a hair's breadth?

A) Slugs
B) Snakes
C) Cockroaches
D) Moles

035

The call of male howler monkeys is so loud it can be heard from how far away?

A) 4.3m/7km
B) 6.8m/11km
C) 8.7m/14km
D) 10m/16km

036

Elephants thump the ground when threatened which can warn other herds. How far can the tremors carry?

A) 31m/50km
B) 15.5m/25km
C) 6.2m/10km
D) 46.6m/75km

Rhinos are not natural predators and shy away from danger, but how are they alerted to oncoming danger?

- **A)** There have inbuilt sensors in their hide
- **B)** Their hearing is very acute
- **C)** The oxpecker birds that eat parasites on the rhinos warn them
- **D)** They feel vibrations through their horn

The loudest recorded lion roar is about as loud as what?

- **A)** A vacuum cleaner (70 decibels)
- **B)** An electric power tool (110 decibels)
- **C)** A jet engine (150 decibels)
- **D)** A truck (80 decibels)

Fire beetles race to lay eggs in charred timber after a forest fire but from how far away can they detect fires?

- **A)** 12.4m/20km
- **B)** 31m/50km
- **C)** 24.8m/40km
- **D)** 18.6m/30km

Polar bears can detect dead seals from how far away?

- **A)** 10m/16km
- **B)** 20m/32.1km
- **C)** 15m/24.1km
- **D)** 5m/8km

041

Why do bulls charge when they see red?

A) Their vision is predominantly black and white but red is the only color they see

B) Red makes them go cross-eyed and this makes them angry

C) Red stimulates the production of adrenaline making them excitable

D) They can't see red at all and just respond to sudden movements

042

What part of their bodies do spiders and crickets hear through?

A) Legs

B) Antenna

C) Thorax

D) Head

043

From how far away can a Peregrine Falcon spot its prey?

A) 5m/8km

B) 10m/16km

C) 15m/24km

D) 20m/32km

044

Which of the following animals does not have a brain?

A) Crab

B) Starfish

C) Octopus

D) History teacher

Which sense does a rattlesnake use to track its prey in the dark?

    A) Sight
    B) Smell
    C) Touch
    D) Heat sensors

046

Which of the following is not a habitat for snakes?

    A) The Arctic
    B) Hawaii
    C) New Zealand
    D) None of the above

047

Barracudas and moray eels have been known to be very aggressive when disturbed and inflict vicious bites on man. Where are they found?

    A) Near reefs and in shallow water
    B) Freshwater rivers
    C) On deep ocean beds
    D) Under toilet seats

048

Which country has the most venomous snakes on the planet?

    A) Russia
    B) Greece
    C) Australia
    D) United Kingdom

049

Where do trapdoor spiders live and capture their prey from?

    A) Trees
    B) Theaters
    C) In mid-air
    D) Underground burrows

Habitat

Which of the following is the least likely place to find ticks?

  A) Wood
  B) Animal fur
  C) Lagoons
  D) Thick vegetation

What creature lays its eggs in moist cowpats?

  A) Turd bird
  B) Stool beetle
  C) Log frog
  D) Dung fly

Where does the Portuguese man o'war live?

  A) North Sea
  B) Atlantic and Mediterranean Oceans
  C) Pacific and Indian Oceans
  D) All oceans

Which animal often shares a burrow with petrels (seabirds), looking after the baby chicks during the day while the mother finds food?

  A) Tuatara
  B) Emperor penguin
  C) Nanny otter
  D) Cuckoo

054

Which of these is a positive result of dams that beavers build?

A) Nothing
B) Soil erosion prevention
C) Water conservation and flood prevention
D) Both B and C

How often do three-toed sloths get down from their trees to have a poo?

    A) Once a day

    B) Once a week

    C) Once every other day

    D) Never, they poo in the tree

055

What gas do domestic livestock, like sheep and cows, emit that contributes to global warming?

    A) Carbon Dioxide

    B) Methane

    C) Hydrogen

    D) Nitrogen

056

How many million tons of methane do domestic livestock emit each year?

    A) 75-95

    B) 35-55

    C) 25-45

    D) 65-85

057

What animal eats exactly the same food as cows but does not produce methane?

    A) Sheep

    B) Goats

    C) Kangaroos

    D) Antelopes

058

Bottoms Up

059

There are so many anchovies off the coast of California that they produce how many times more waste than the population of Los Angeles?

A) 10
B) 20
C) 100
D) 500

060

In its lifetime, a chicken can produce enough waste to produce enough electricity to do what?

A) Run an electric car for a year
B) Supply a household for a week
C) Light up the Empire State Building for a year
D) Power a 100 watt lightbulb for five hours

061

What is the most common form of death among fruit flies?

A) Constipation
B) Diarrhea
C) Suffocating in poo in which they've landed
D) Eating infected faeces

062

In a farting competition which of these animals would be crowned champion?

A) Cow
B) Rhinoceros
C) Skunk
D) Elephant

Teeth

Why do long-eared bats have very sharp teeth?
- **A)** To take bites out of large mammals
- **B)** They bare their teeth to attract females
- **C)** To crunch moths
- **D)** To hold onto branches while they sleep

How many teeth does a wolf have?
- **A)** 28
- **B)** 42
- **C)** 36
- **D)** 32

How many teeth does the great grey slug have?
- **A)** 60
- **B)** 124
- **C)** 24,000
- **D)** 28,000

How many teeth do snails have?
- **A)** 42
- **B)** 17,600
- **C)** 25,600
- **D)** They don't have teeth

067

How many teeth do elephants have?

- **A)** 0
- **B)** 36
- **C)** Only 2 but they never stop growing
- **D)** Only 4 at a time but they have 5 sets of replacements

068

How many rows of teeth does a shark have?

- **A)** 1
- **B)** 12
- **C)** 16
- **D)** 2

Records

What is the fastest marine animal?
- **A)** Tiger shark
- **B)** Cheetah fish
- **C)** Killer whale
- **D)** Conga eel

069

What is the fastest flying bird?
- **A)** Bald eagle
- **B)** Albatross
- **C)** Peregrine falcon
- **D)** Hawk

070

Which animal has the largest nerve fibers?
- **A)** Hippo
- **B)** Blue whale
- **C)** Giant squid
- **D)** Elephant

071

Sea wasps are jellyfish with 15feet/4.5m long tentacles. How big are their bodies?
- **A)** The size of a pin
- **B)** The size of a basketball
- **C)** The size of a tennis ball
- **D)** The size of a car

072

073

Who's the biggest of the big cats?

- **A)** The Lion
- **B)** The Mountain Lion
- **C)** The Black Panther
- **D)** The Siberian Tiger

074

What's the biggest animal that has ever lived?

- **A)** White elephant
- **B)** Mammoth
- **C)** Blue whale
- **D)** Tyrannosaurus rex

075

At what speed can a cheetah pursue its prey?

- **A)** 120mph/193.1kph
- **B)** 60mph/96.5kph
- **C)** 20mph/32.2kph
- **D)** 5mph/8kph

076

To what length can the venomous Scolopendra giant centipede grow?

- **A)** 12in/30cm
- **B)** 6in/15.2cm
- **C)** 3in/7.6cm
- **D)** 3.3ft/1m

Which member of the snake family has the longest fangs?

    A) Monkey cobra
    B) Montgomery python
    C) Black adder
    D) Gaboon viper

How large are giant squids from head to tentacle-end?

    A) 8-11m/26-36ft
    B) 5-8m/16-26ft
    C) 15-18m/49-59ft
    D) 20-23m/65-75ft

Which of the following is the least dangerous animal to humans?

    A) Wolf
    B) Cougar
    C) Puma
    D) Mountain lion

Fleas can jump up to how many times their body length?

    A) 40
    B) 30
    C) 20
    D) 10

081

A roadrunner will travel at great speed to catch a lizard or a snake but how fast can it run?

A) 6mph/10kph
B) 10mph/16kph
C) 33mph/53kph
D) 23mph/37kph

082

How big was the largest recorded komodo dragon?

A) About as heavy as a newly born baby
B) About as heavy as a fully grown man
C) About as heavy as a small car
D) About as heavy as a truck

083

How many species of cockroach are there?

A) 4500
B) 3500
C) 2500
D) 1000

084

How long have cockroaches been in existence?

A) 100 million years
B) 200 million years
C) 250 million years
D) 300 million years

Up to what length can the great Amazonian leech grow?

A) 12in/30cm
B) 18in/46cm
C) 24in/60cm
D) 30in/76cm

Catholic and flat-headed frogs can store water in their bladders and can survive droughts for up to how long?

A) 1 year
B) 5 years
C) 7 years
D) 10 years

How many species of snake are found in Great Britain?

A) 0
B) 1
C) 3
D) 5

Which snake, found in Great Britain, is venomous?

A) Grass snake
B) Adder
C) Smooth snake
D) Feather boa

089

How many species of scorpion are there?

- **A)** 600
- **B)** 1200
- **C)** 1500
- **D)** 2400

090

Which of these can jump up to 3 meters in the air?

- **A)** Frosby lizard
- **B)** Swing-backed toad
- **C)** Goliath frog
- **D)** Moses hopper cat

091

Which animal feature has the fastest growing cells ever recorded?

- **A)** Cockroach exoskeleton
- **B)** Lizard tails
- **C)** Moose antlers
- **D)** Starfish arms

092

How fast can hippos run on land?

- **A)** 35mph/56kph
- **B)** 45mph/72kph
- **C)** 10mph/16kph
- **D)** 20mph/32kph

Which is the largest predatory fish?

    A) Killer whale
    B) Hammerhead Shark
    C) Great White Shark
    D) Barracuda

094

All of these animals, except one, scavenges for its food. Which one?

A) Hyena
B) Camel
C) Crow
D) Vulture

095

What animal eats more than any other?

A) Blue Whale
B) Elephant
C) Lion
D) Great White Shark

096

How many tons of food does the Blue Whale eat per day?

A) 2
B) 7
C) 4
D) 10

097

Tarantulas have very large fangs for biting victims. What is their favored prey?

A) Human beings and cows
B) Birds, mice and lizards
C) Snakes
D) Fish

Eating

How does a fly eat?

A) It has a special straw-like attachment on its abdomen which sucks the food straight in

B) It lifts food with its front two legs into its mouth

C) It vomits on food to dissolve it and then slurps it up

D) Its bum has two uses and can suck food in as well as pooing

In Florida, people are advised not to go near water at dusk. Why?

A) It's when the alligators are feeding

B) The cooling water gives off toxic gas

C) To keep away from mosquitoes

D) Flash floods often occur at dusk

Which of the following does a termite NOT munch through?

A) Wood

B) Bricks

C) Concrete

D) Plastic

What insects eat furniture?

A) Furniture beetles

B) Woodlice

C) Chippendale flies

D) Wardrobe beetle

102 How long do snakes chew for before swallowing their food?

    A) An hour

    B) A day

    C) A week

    D) Snakes can't chew. They have to digest their prey whole

103 What human food is a mealworm partial to?

    A) Cheese

    B) Flour

    C) Sugar

    D) Chocolate

104 Tsetse flies can drink so much blood that after a hearty meal they can barely fly, but how many times their own weight can they drink?

    A) 3

    B) 2

    C) 1

    D) 6

105 What are a house mouse's favorite foodstuffs?

    A) Cheese

    B) Cereals and chocolate

    C) Seeds and nuts

    D) B and C

What do clothes moths eat?

A) Feathers

B) Fur

C) Wool

D) All of the above

The fiercest animals in the Arctic are polar bears. What is their favored prey?

A) Seals

B) Penguins

C) Humans

D) Fish

Why do elephants raid ripe paddy and finger millet plants?

A) Because the plants have higher levels of protein, calcium and sodium than their normal diet of wild grasses

B) Because when ripe, the plants emit a smell similar to female elephants

C) Because the plants taste like mangoes

D) They eat anything that gets in their way

Mice will eat anything left out and have been known to eat which of the following?

A) Soap

B) Candles

C) Cereal

D) All of the above

110 Ground squirrels don't always eat nuts and acorns. What else is vulnerable?

A) Wild grasses
B) Fruit trees
C) Flowerheads
D) Fledglings

111 How do skuas and frigate birds obtain food?

A) They dive for fish in shallow waters
B) They attack fish-eating birds and coerce them into dropping food
C) They eat the eggs of other birds
D) They scavenge in trashcans

112 The etruscan shrew has to eat how often just to survive?

A) Every hour
B) Every 12 hours
C) Every 4 hours
D) Every 2 hours

113 Eagles have been known to grab which of the following animals?

A) Foals
B) Calves
C) Lambs
D) Piglets

Why do hens swallow grit and small stones?

A) They have terrible eyesight

B) They swallow the small stones to grind up the food in their stomach

C) The stones, when broken down, release a vital trace element

D) They're stupid

114

What do some ribbon worms do if they cannot find food?

A) They hibernate for weeks at a time until food sources improve

B) They eat themselves

C) They adapt and eat plants like seaweed

D) They nibble at pebbles to fill their stomachs and regurgitate them when food comes along

115

Which bird can eat only when its head is upside-down?

A) Flamingo

B) Albatross

C) Ostrich

D) Hummingbird

116

Which of these does the kea parrot like to eat?

A) Sand

B) The flesh of dead sheep

C) Other parrots' poo

D) Cows' eyeballs

117

118 **H**ow long can vampire bats go without feeding?
- **A)** 21 days
- **B)** 14 days
- **C)** 7 days
- **D)** 2 days

119 **T**he maggots of blow flies are bloodsuckers. Where do they feed?
- **A)** They hook themselves onto human toes
- **B)** They hook themselves onto human fingers
- **C)** They hook themselves onto human mouths and noses
- **D)** They burrow under clothing and latch onto human stomachs

120 **V**ultures eat carrion but what is carrion?
- **A)** Paralysed animals
- **B)** A type of fruit
- **C)** Bones of dead animals
- **D)** Rotting flesh

If attacked by a bird, how do swallowtail caterpillars defend themselves?

- **A)** By vomiting a foul-smelling corrosive liquid
- **B)** By shooting out spikes from their spine
- **C)** By emitting a shrill scream
- **D)** By rolling up in a ball

How do gemsboks defend themselves against lions?

- **A)** They stab the lions with their dagger-like horns
- **B)** The gemsboks rear up on their hind legs and hit out with their hooves
- **C)** They blind the lions by kicking dust in their eyes
- **D)** The gemsboks spit acid

Which sea urchin has ultra-sharp spines that break off in an enemy's flesh causing great pain?

- **A)** Pin cushion sea urchin
- **B)** Hat pin sea urchin
- **C)** Lancer sea urchin
- **D)** Speared sea urchin

Cape buffaloes are so aggressive they can fend off what?

- **A)** Elephants
- **B)** Lions
- **C)** Mosquitoes
- **D)** Ticks

125 The pangolin has so many scales it looks like a fir cone but what does it do if a predator is not discouraged by its armor?

    A) It rolls up in a ball

    B) It runs away

    C) It squirts a pungent liquid

    D) Its scales change color to show anger

126 If a silverfish is bitten by a predator, how does it get away?

    A) Its scales are slippery so a predator can't hold it

    B) Its scales are waxy and they just come off in the predator's mouth

    C) Their scales taste bitter which makes the predator drop them

    D) It spits a corrosive liquid onto the predator's tongue

127 What defense mechanism does a platypus employ when attacked?

    A) It grabs hold of the attacker and crushes it with its beak

    B) It has poisonous spines on the back of each ankle and kicks out at the attacker, injecting poison

    C) It tries to drown its attacker by holding it underwater

    D) It lashes out with its tail using it like a whip

What does the Texas Horned Lizard do to frighten off predators?

   A) Squirts acid from its horns

   B) Squirts venom from a gland at the base of its tail

   C) Squirts blood from its eyes

   D) Spits venom from its mouth

How do clownfish avoid their enemies?

   A) They spit at them

   B) They ride on the backs of sharks

   C) They swim amongst the stinging tentacles of sea anemones

   D) They camouflage themselves in coral reefs

What do fishermen in the Sundarbans do to repel the tigers?

   A) Leave out scarecrows doused in human scent so that they will be attacked

   B) Wear masks on the back of their heads because tigers don't usually attack human faces

   C) Release pigs into the wild so that the tigers will eat them instead

   D) All of the above

131 **W**here is a scorpion's stinger?

- **A)** At the tip of its tail
- **B)** At the root of its tail
- **C)** On the top of its head
- **D)** On its back legs

132 **H**yenas are mostly scavengers but in packs they will attack wildebeest, zebras and sometimes lions. How do they challenge their prey?

- **A)** By running them down
- **B)** By lining up in rows so the prey cannot pass
- **C)** By circling them and wearing them down
- **D)** By jumping on sleeping animals

133 **H**ow many shark attacks occur around the world every year?

- **A)** Around 1
- **B)** Less than 100
- **C)** Around 5,000
- **D)** More than 10,000

134 **W**hen do bee attacks generally occur?

- **A)** When you eat honey outdoors
- **B)** When you stumble on a nest
- **C)** When you swim in natural lagoons
- **D)** When you pick flowers whose pollen bees want

Since 1970, on average, how many mountain lion attacks on humans have there been?

A) 4
B) 14
C) 34
D) 44

Wolves hunt in packs but how do they subdue their prey?

A) They all watch while one suffocates the prey
B) They simultaneously jump on the victims back
C) One goes for the throat while the others go for the underbelly
D) One slashes the hind legs while another holds the nose down

The whiptail scorpion does not sting an assailant. What does it do to deter its attacker?

A) It squirts vinegar
B) It lashes out with its tail
C) It squirts a toxic venom
D) It plays dead

How many confirmed shark attacks have there been on humans between 1580 and 2002?

A) Just over 200
B) Just over 1000
C) Just over 2000
D) Just over 5000

135

136

137

138

139

What is the Komodo dragon's preferred method of kill?

A) Snapping the throat of its prey
B) Clawing a hole in the prey's stomach
C) Clawing the back of the prey's legs
D) Using its weight to hold the prey down

How many million dollars worth of damage does a termite cause each year in New Orleans?

140

A) 26
B) 158
C) 200
D) 300

Each year rats eat what percentage of the world's crops?

141

A) 1%
B) 5%
C) 20%
D) 80%

Which tiny invertebrates are capable of making a house collapse?

142

A) Termites
B) Stick insects
C) Ants
D) Fleas

Which animals are known to smash up cars in the search of food?

143

A) Monkeys
B) Giraffes
C) Black bears
D) Meerkats

144

Why are Quelea birds regarded as pests?

A) They carry disease fatal to man

B) They are attracted to mucus and have been known to peck at people's eyes

C) They attack domesticated animals

D) They eat whole fields of grain in one sitting

145

If a beaver dam has been built in the wrong location what is a natural result?

A) Nothing

B) Abundant harvests

C) Flooding

D) Tree shortages

146

The maggots of the new world screw worm are flesh eaters. In 1976 how many dollars worth of livestock were destroyed by it?

A) 600m

B) 500m

C) 400m

D) 300m

147

Every year, in the USA, they spend half a billion dollars doing what?

A) Inoculating people against killer bees

B) Cleaning bird poo off statues

C) Killing cockroaches

D) Making scarecrows

Which beetle causes irreparable damage to potatoes and other winter vegetables?

A) Colorado beetle

B) Ten-line june beetle

C) Rose weevil

D) Longhorn beetle

148

Thousands of trees in New York and Chicago have been destroyed by Asian long-horned beetles. What kind of tree have they been munching?

A) Oak

B) Elm

C) Maple

D) Beech

149

How do you tell the difference between plant damage caused by deer or that caused by rabbits?

A) Rabbits leave plants with a jagged break. Deer leave plants with a clean break

B) Deer leave plants with a jagged break. Rabbits leave plants with a clean break

C) Rabbits only eat the leaves but deer eat the whole plant

D) Deer leave their slobber everywhere which smells of onions

150

151

When do camels spit?

A) When they show affection
B) When they're angry
C) When they have run a long way
D) When they're hungry

152

Which groups of people are most at risk of becoming a crocodile's dinner?

A) Fishermen
B) People washing on riverbanks
C) Water-gatherers
D) All of the above

153

Which groups of people are most at risk if bitten by scorpions?

A) Women
B) Tall people
C) Young and elderly
D) Everyone

154

Honey bees' stings are not very toxic. How many times would a healthy person need to be stung to be at risk of dying?

A) Over 5000
B) Over 100
C) Over 1000
D) Over 2000

Take Care

In the US state of California, on average one person dies every year from what?

- **A)** Swallowing a wasp
- **B)** Being crushed by a grizzly bear
- **C)** Pushed off a mountain by a goat
- **D)** Being gored by a mountain lion

155

If camping near black bear territory, what should you never leave outside your tent?

- **A)** Food
- **B)** Clothes
- **C)** Fire
- **D)** Sleeping bags

156

Why are sea bass dangerous?

- **A)** Because they can swim up your bum and eat your insides
- **B)** Because they can take an entire arm off with one bite
- **C)** Because they can paralyse a human in five seconds with their poisonous spines
- **D)** Because they can swim very fast around you and disorientate you

157

What should be taken to combat a severe reaction to a bee sting?

- **A)** Anti-coagulant
- **B)** Pheromones
- **C)** Antihistamine
- **D)** Vitamin B

158

159 **W**hich of the following is more likely to happen than being bitten by a black widow?

    A) Striking oil in your back garden

    B) Getting struck by lightning

    C) Learning that you're in line for the British throne

    D) Your hair turning grey overnight

160 **I**n areas where fire ants are prevalent and nip people in swarms, like parts of Texas, people are advised not to do what?

    A) Eat outdoors

    B) Sit on the ground

    C) Stand still for long periods

    D) All of the above

161 **W**hat has not been found in a beaver dam?

    A) Television aerial

    B) Railway sleepers

    C) Ballpoint pens

    D) Deer antlers

162 **H**ow do the Masai tribe frighten off lions?

    A) They cover themselves in dung to repel the lions

    B) They wear lion skins to demonstrate their territory

    C) They hit them with sticks

    D) They shake cowbells

Take Care

163

Which animal brought the construction of a railway line, from Uganda to the Indian Ocean, to a halt when he killed the Police Superintendent who was asleep in a train carriage?

A) Tiger

B) Lion

C) Elephant

D) Rhino

164

In the town of Churchill, Canada, they've built what?

A) A retirement home for husky dogs

B) A hospital for grizzly bears

C) A prison for polar bears

D) A hotel for seals

165

In the sixteenth century, in Scotland, you would often see spittals at the side of the road. What were they?

A) Dog baths

B) Stables

C) Shelters in which to hide from wolves

D) Pits for dead horses

166 The people of Madagascar are terrified of a creature called an aye-aye. What is it?

A) A snake with big bulbous eyes
B) A giant lizard with a revolving head
C) A primate with weird bendy fingers
D) A bear with fur that glows in the dark

167 If escaping from a crocodile, why should you not climb a tree?

A) The trees in crocodile swamps have unstable roots and could fall in the water
B) Crocodiles can climb trees
C) Crocodiles can jump into the tree
D) The trees have poisonous sap

168 A single gopher can be a major pest with its gnawing behavior. Which of the following has it been known to chew through?

A) Vines
B) Water pipes
C) Lawn sprinkler system
D) All of the above

169 Which breed of dog was used as a bodyguard for horse-drawn carriages to protect against highwaymen?

A) German Shepherd
B) Doberman Pinscher
C) Dalmatian
D) St Bernard

170

What should you do if a crocodile attacks you and grabs you in its mouth?

- **A)** Tickle it between the nostrils and it will let you go
- **B)** Poke it between the eyes and it lets go
- **C)** Start crying because it hates the taste of salt
- **D)** Go limp and it thinks you're dead already and lets go

171

Tourists have been found gored by buffaloes. One single sweep of their horns can split a man from groin to sternum, but when will buffaloes stalk humans without reason?

- **A)** When they are old and rheumatic
- **B)** When it's full moon
- **C)** When they are wounded
- **D)** When they mistake a human for a lion

172

People have been known to catch headlice from doing what?

- **A)** Sharing hats
- **B)** Borrowing stuffed toys
- **C)** Listening to other people's headphones
- **D)** All of the above

173 **W**hich distinctive animal ran ahead of fire engines to warn people of fire and is now the mascot for the fire service?

    A) Llama

    B) Shetland pony

    C) Dalmatian

    D) Panther

174 **W**hy are elephants deemed most dangerous in December and January?

    A) Because they traditionally raid crops at this time

    B) Because it's mating season

    C) Because they give birth at that time

    D) Because the hot weather makes them cantankerous

175

African tribes believe leopards have magical properties. A stare from one can cause a monkey to fall out of a tree dead. What is the probable cause of this phenomenon?

A) Leopards cast the evil eye on them

B) The monkey has a heart attack and dies of fright

C) Pure coincidence

D) The monkey sacrifices itself so the leopard won't attack the colony

176

For what purpose do African tribes use the chopped-up whiskers of leopards?

A) They wear them to frighten off invaders

B) They use them in a spell to bring back lost tribesmen

C) They believe they give you better night sight

D) They use them as a poison – it causes peritonitis

177

What do Madagascan people think will happen if an aye-aye points its middle finger at you?

A) That you are marked by the devil

B) That you will turn into a zombie

C) That you will die swiftly and horribly

D) That you will never have children

178 According to African folklore how have gorillas defeated leopards?

    A) By squeezing their throats until they are asphyxiated

    B) By swinging them above their heads until their tail comes off

    C) By clawing their eyes out

    D) They never have

---

179 Where is the phoenix legend supposed to have originated?

    A) Starlings and crows sitting on smoking chimneys and fumigating their feathers

    B) Birds of the crow family stealing burning embers

    C) Jackdaws and magpies proffering their chests to burning flames

    D) All of the above

---

180 In Tanzanian folklore, which animal was created by the devil from the tail of a monkey, the skin of a crocodile, the tongue of a toad and the horns of a rhino?

    A) Skink

    B) Chameleon

    C) Pit viper

    D) Komodo dragon

Folklore

In Mbugwe folklore, which animals are regarded as witches' familiars?

- **A)** Panthers
- **B)** Leopards
- **C)** Hyenas
- **D)** Raccoons

Panthers have been regarded as dangerous and in 1997 in Kenya they were blamed for several killings but who is most likely accountable for the unexplained deaths?

- **A)** Buffaloes
- **B)** Jackals
- **C)** Humans
- **D)** Hornets

The Egyptian god of the dead was symbolized with the head of which animal?

- **A)** Vulture
- **B)** Jackal
- **C)** Elephant
- **D)** Lion

Which bird, deemed a bad omen for sailors, has the largest wing span?

- **A)** Albatross
- **B)** Peregrine Falcon
- **C)** Hummingbird
- **D)** Bald Eagle

185

What percentage of mosquitoes carry a disease that could be fatal to humans?

A) 1%
B) 0.1%
C) 0.001%
D) 11%

186

Some people are allergic to animal dandruff. What is the dandruff called?

A) Mititis
B) Animalitis
C) Dander
D) Danderuff

187

Ticks are bloodsuckers and natural hosts to disease. Once a tick gets its teeth into you, how long does it take for the tick to transmit disease organisms into your body?

A) 6 hours
B) 3 hours
C) 1 hour
D) 10 hours

188

Apart from malaria what diseases do mosquitoes carry?

A) Dengue and yellow fever
B) Encephalitis and elephantiasis
C) All of the above
D) None of the above

Disease

How many disease-causing organisms and parasites are spread by houseflies?

A) 20
B) 200
C) 400
D) 600

189

Which of these can give you the deadly disease of sleeping sickness?

A) Tsetse flies
B) Houseflies
C) Mosquitoes
D) Leeches

190

Sleeping sickness is caused by a parasite where it enters the central nervous system causing deep coma and death. How many people in Central Africa die each year from it?

A) 250-300
B) 2500-3000
C) 250,000-300,000
D) 2,500,000-3,000,000

191

Which animals were responsible for spreading the Black Death across Europe?

A) Dogs
B) Rats
C) Cats
D) Mice

192

193 About how many cases of bubonic plague are there in the USA every year?

- **A)** 0
- **B)** 4
- **C)** 13
- **D)** 22

194 Creutzfeldt-Jacob disease is the human form of which disease?

- **A)** Mad cow disease
- **B)** Foot and mouth disease
- **C)** Hog cholera
- **D)** Rabies

195 Tetanus spores are found in the poo of which animals?

- **A)** Sheep and horses
- **B)** Cats and dogs
- **C)** Rats and guinea pigs
- **D)** All of the above

196 Cockroaches can transmit the bacteria that cause which kind of food poisoning?

- **A)** Salmonella
- **B)** Ecoli
- **C)** Ehrlichiosis
- **D)** Listeria

Which one of the following diseases is transmitted by animals to humans?

197

A) Mad Fish Disease
B) Rabbit fever
C) Tapeworm
D) All of the above

What is the term given to diseases transmitted to humans via animals?

198

A) Animotic
B) Zoonotic
C) Animaloid
D) Zoonoid

What percentage of the world's population has malaria?

199

A) 10
B) 50
C) 25
D) 1

What disease can be transmitted by cat fleas?

200

A) Mononucleosis
B) Toxic Shock Syndrome
C) Ringworm
D) Murine typhus

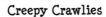

Creepy Crawlies

201

Which of the following statements is NOT true?

- **A)** A leech is a parasite
- **B)** Parasites live on or inside other organisms
- **C)** They feed off their host
- **D)** They are always beneficial to their host organism

202

Scorpions in the jungles of Central America and Southern Africa can grow to what length?

- **A)** 30cm
- **B)** 20cm
- **C)** 10cm
- **D)** 50cm

203

Tarantulas have very large fangs for biting victims. What is their favored prey?

- **A)** Birds, mice and lizards
- **B)** Human beings and cows
- **C)** Snakes
- **D)** Fish

204

Widow spiders come in various colors. Which of the following does not exist?

- **A)** Black in the USA
- **B)** Red in the Middle East
- **C)** Brown in Australia
- **D)** White in Asia

Creepy Crawlies

What is the usual reaction to a scorpion sting?

A) Immediate death
B) Local pain and swelling
C) Itchy rash
D) Numbing cold

Which of the following is true about centipedes?

A) Some varieties have a poisonous bite
B) Some varieties have sharp claws which can dig in and puncture your skin causing infection
C) Both statements
D) Neither statement

Which widow spiders have a venomous bite?

A) Male only
B) Both male and female
C) Neither male nor female
D) Female only

Some poisonous millipedes squirt which highly toxic substance?

A) Saline
B) Cyanide
C) Fluoride
D) Arsenic

Creepy Crawlies

209

In order to surprise its prey, different types of crab spider can disguise themselves to look like all of the following things, except for one. Which is the odd one out?

A) Tree bark
B) A shoe
C) A dried leaf
D) A bird dropping

210

How many locusts are there in an average swarm?

A) 4-8,000
B) 40-80 million
C) 4-8 million
D) 400-800 million

211

How much food can one locust eat per day?

A) 2 grams
B) 1 gram
C) 0.5 grams
D) 5 grams

212

Furniture beetles lay their larvae in damp wood which the larvae eat on hatching. What do we know the larvae as?

A) Woodlice
B) Woodworm
C) Fleas
D) Ticks

Creepy Crawlies

How many offspring can one pair of cockroaches have in one year?

A) 1 million
B) 1000
C) 10,000
D) 100,000

Which mosquitoes suck blood?

A) Only males
B) Both males and females
C) Only females
D) Neither

The daddy-long-legs spider has venom more deadly than that of a black widow, but why do they not bite humans?

A) They don't like the taste
B) They never come into contact with humans
C) They don't produce enough quantities
D) Their jaws aren't big enough

Cars parked under trees are sometimes spotted by a sugary liquid called honeydew. Which animal produces this honeydew?

A) Aphids
B) Houseflies
C) Lacewings
D) Ants

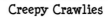

217 Their eggs are carried by mosquitoes and drop off into human flesh on contact. The maggots then grow in the flesh and eat their way out on maturity. What are they?

- **A)** Bot flies
- **B)** Tsetse flies
- **C)** Colorado beetles
- **D)** Saturnid moth

218 Why do deathwatch beetles strike their heads against wood?

- **A)** To warn others of impending danger
- **B)** As a mating call
- **C)** To dislodge tiny mites in the wood that they eat
- **D)** To mark territory

219 How many stomachs do leeches have?

- **A)** 1
- **B)** 10
- **C)** 4
- **D)** 2

220 Flies' legs are covered in hair so attract plenty of germs and dirt. How often do they wash?

- **A)** Once a day
- **B)** Once a week
- **C)** Never
- **D)** Once a month

How many noses do slugs have?

    A) 2
    B) 4
    C) 6
    D) 8

Redbacks were the last spider for which an antivenin was discovered. What year was it made?

    A) 1946
    B) 1956
    C) 1976
    D) 1986

223 **A**n electric eel can produce a shock large enough to knock a horse off its feet. How many volts is this?

- **A)** 200
- **B)** 400
- **C)** 800
- **D)** 1600

224 **T**he black angler fish has a glowing lantern-like object on its nose to lure prey. What makes it glow?

- **A)** It eats radioactive fish
- **B)** It is actually another fish that lives off the food debris
- **C)** The object is made up of glowing bacteria
- **D)** It produces chemicals that glow on fusion

225 **W**hat is distinctive about the bite of a blue-ringed octopus?

- **A)** It gives you an electric shock
- **B)** Their bite leaves two puncture wounds, like vampire bats
- **C)** It leaves a jagged scar
- **D)** They bite so softly people don't realize

226 **W**hat is the most dangerous freshwater fish?

- **A)** Stingray
- **B)** Blue shark
- **C)** Piranha
- **D)** Marlin

Spooky Sea Creatures

Which one of these sharks is NOT a man eater?

A) The Great White Shark
B) The Tiger Shark
C) Sharks are not man-eaters
D) The Bull Shark

227

Which jellyfish is considered one of the deadliest creatures on the planet?

A) Bag jellyfish
B) Box jellyfish
C) Sack jellyfish
D) Green jellyfish

228

How does the venomous stonefish camouflage itself?

A) It matches the color of the seabed
B) It hides under the sand
C) It hides inside whales' mouths
D) It can change its shape to look like harmless angel fish

229

On July 20, 2002, a female squid washed up on the shore of Tasmania with bite marks on her neck. How did she get them?

A) She fought with a fisherman who bit her to force her to release him
B) It was part of a courting ritual
C) She had been bitten by a shark
D) A seal bit her when she washed up

230

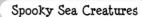

Spooky Sea Creatures

231 The Arawana fish is renowned for its jumping skills. It can jump up to 2 meters/6.5 feet out of the water but why?

    A) When they're short of oxygen

    B) As part of its courtship display

    C) To swim upstream

    D) To feed on the small birds and bats in the overhanging trees

232 The lionfish can deliver poisonous stings from its spines. Where are they located?

    A) Along its back and fins

    B) Around its mouth

    C) On top of its head

    D) All around its tail

233 In a blue-ringed octopus its venom glands are as big as its what?

    A) Brain

    B) Tentacles

    C) Eyes

    D) Mouth

234 How do sea urchins move?

    A) They don't move

    B) They walk on the tips of their teeth

    C) They walk on their spines

    D) They propel themselves to roll along

Spooky Sea Creatures

Where is the heart of a Shrimp located?

235

- **A)** It doesn't have a heart
- **B)** Tail
- **C)** Thorax
- **D)** Head

Which of the following can turn its stomach inside out?

236

- **A)** Octopus
- **B)** Crab
- **C)** Starfish
- **D)** Sea Cow

Whose tongue weighs more than an elephant?

237

- **A)** Blue whale
- **B)** Killer whale
- **C)** Whale shark
- **D)** Manatee

What color is the blood of lobsters?

238

- **A)** Lilac
- **B)** Red
- **C)** Pale blue
- **D)** Yellow

239 Falcons, eagles, owls and hawks are all what type of birds?

A) Seabirds

B) Flightless birds

C) Songbirds

D) Birds of prey

240 Where do cuckoos lay their eggs?

A) In tree nests they make out of twigs

B) Amongst the long grasses in sand dunes

C) In smaller birds' nests

D) In nests that other birds have deserted

241 Why do some barn owls glow at night?

A) They possess magical qualities

B) The animals they've eaten are irradiated

C) They eat glow-worms

D) The trees they roost in are full of the phosphorescent spores of honey fungus

Bad Birds

Which US president wanted the turkey as the national emblem and not the eagle because he said the eagle was a bird of "bad moral character" living by "sharping and robbing".

A) Thomas Jefferson
B) George Washington
C) Benjamin Franklin
D) Abraham Lincoln

What do turkeys do to members of their flock who are different or inferior?

A) Peck them to death
B) Protect them and give them food
C) Hound them out of the flock
D) Pull their wing feathers out

When African Grey Parrots are nervous, how do they behave?

A) They hide under a wing
B) They blink rapidly
C) They bite their nails
D) They scratch their ears

Which is the only bird that can fly backwards?

A) Wren
B) Hummingbird
C) Kestrel
D) Hawk

246 What is the common behavior for a cuckoo hatchling?

    A) They fly out of the nest within an hour

    B) They push out all the other hatchlings and take food off surrogate parents

    C) They help feed the other hatchlings

    D) They kill the parents in order to keep the nest

247 How many birds die every year, on average, from smashing into windows?

    A) 1000

    B) 5000

    C) 7000

    D) 10,000

Sneaky Snakes

What snakes are the most poisonous snakes in the world?

- **A)** Vipers
- **B)** Rattlesnakes
- **C)** Sea snakes
- **D)** Pythons

What does the spitting cobra spit?

- **A)** Blood
- **B)** Food
- **C)** Venom
- **D)** Bile

What is snake venom's main component?

- **A)** Urine
- **B)** Bile
- **C)** Mucus
- **D)** Saliva

How can a red garter snake survive after being attacked by crows?

- **A)** The crows eat its liver and it can regenerate its liver
- **B)** The crows only eat its eyes and it can function when blinded
- **C)** Its taste is repulsive so the crows will only peck momentarily
- **D)** It does not survive

252 How many people are bitten by venomous snakes every year?

- **A)** Between 5 and 12
- **B)** About 70
- **C)** About 700
- **D)** About 7000

253 How many of these die?

- **A)** About 7000
- **B)** About 70
- **C)** Between 5 and 12
- **D)** About 700

254 What part of a snakes body detects sound?

- **A)** Top of its head
- **B)** Jawbone
- **C)** Tip of its tongue
- **D)** Tail

255 There are 2,700 species of snakes but what percentage are NOT venomous?

- **A)** More than 20%
- **B)** More than 50%
- **C)** More than 70%
- **D)** More than 80%

Which of these is not a reptile?

A) Skink
B) Chuckwalla
C) Malachai
D) Galliwasp

The saltwater crocodile can grow up to how long?

A) Over 30 feet/9 meters long
B) Over 25 feet/7.5 meters long
C) Over 20 feet/6 meters long
D) Over 15 feet/4.5 meters long

258 How does a blind chameleon adapt to its environment?

A) It teams up with a seeing chameleon who sends messages on which color to change

B) It still automatically changes color with its environment

C) It lives in one place so that it doesn't have to change color

D) It hides in burrows

259 How fast can an average 100lb Komodo dragon eat a 40lb pig?

A) 7 minutes
B) 10 minutes
C) 17 minutes
D) 23 minutes

260 What is the most deadly part of a Komodo dragon?

A) Claws
B) Incisors
C) Mouth bacteria
D) Whipping tail

Rotten Reptiles

The Gila monster is one of only two venomous lizards. What is the other one?

A) Iguana
B) Horned Lizard
C) Mexican Bearded Lizard
D) Skink

261

How does the Gila Monster introduce venom into its victim?

A) The venom is held in two sacs above its fangs which burst on contact with a victim
B) Its teeth have two grooves that conduct the venom from glands in the lower jaw into the wound as the lizard chews on its victim
C) Its saliva is venomous so any contact with its mouth will cause a reaction
D) The venom is triggered by the tongue hitting the roof of its mouth when it bites a victim

262

How do crocodiles kill their prey?

A) By flicking their tail and knocking the victim down
B) By injecting venom
C) By inflicting wounds that cause massive blood loss
D) By rolling them around underwater until they drown

263

264

How far away from a skunk should you stand so as not to get sprayed with its foul stench?

A) 4 feet/1.2 meters
B) 8 feet/2.4 meters
C) 12 feet/3.6 meters
D) One mile/1.6 km

265

Giraffes have the same number of neck bones as humans. How many do they have?

A) 3
B) 7
C) 21
D) 28

266

When frightened or wounded, elephants can charge and trample people underfoot. How many miles per hour can they run?

A) 30
B) 40
C) 50
D) 60

267

A Siberian tiger can weigh up to 350kg. In the wild 13 men tried to lift an adult gaur (type of ox) but could not budge it. A Siberian tiger came along and dragged it off. How far?

A) 2km/1.2 miles
B) 1km/0.6 miles
C) 37 meters/121 feet
D) 12 meters/39 feet

Menacing Mammals

In an area of the Indian subcontinent known as the Sundarbans an average of how many people, mostly fishermen, are killed by tigers every year?

A) 12
B) 60
C) 36
D) 90

268

How does a tiger kill its prey?

A) By biting the back of the neck and severing the spinal cord
B) By biting the victim's throat and suffocating it
C) Both of the above
D) Neither of the above

269

What behavior do bears exhibit when they are about to charge?

A) They wave their tails from side to side
B) They lift their arms above their head
C) They lay their ears back
D) They roll their eyes

270

How many spines are there on a hedgehog?

A) 1000
B) 500
C) 12,000
D) 7000

271

272 How do vampire bats keep their victim's blood flowing?

A) They suck so hard the blood doesn't have a chance to clot

B) They repeatedly pierce the skin

C) They have anticoagulants on their teeth

D) They only suck for a few seconds and then move onto the next victim

273 What Antipodean animal has one of the strongest jaws and devours all of its prey, including fur bones and tails?

A) Kangaroo

B) Tasmanian devil

C) Wombat

D) Duck-billed platypus

274 How far can hippos open their mouths?

A) 2 feet/61 cm

B) 8 feet/ 2.4 meters

C) 6 feet/3.3 meters

D) 4 feet/1.2 meters

Us and Them

Annually about how many people die from scorpion stings worldwide?

- **A)** None
- **B)** Under 10
- **C)** Several hundred
- **D)** Several thousand

Within the confines of the Serengeti National Park in Tanzania, which animals cause most human fatalities?

- **A)** Humans
- **B)** Elephants
- **C)** Cape Buffaloes
- **D)** Lions

In North America in the past 100 years how many people have been killed by black bears?

- **A)** 4
- **B)** 40
- **C)** 14
- **D)** 403

How many people were believed killed by grizzly bears in Alaska in the year 2000?

- **A)** 2
- **B)** 3
- **C)** 8
- **D)** 10

275

276

277

278

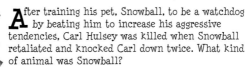

279

After training his pet, Snowball, to be a watchdog by beating him to increase his aggressive tendencies, Carl Hulsey was killed when Snowball retaliated and knocked Carl down twice. What kind of animal was Snowball?

A) A goat

B) A cow

C) A sheep

D) A horse

280

How did 'killer bees' come into being?

A) Bees were bred in Japan with an extra chromosome to increase aggression in 1990

B) Bee and wasp genes were combined in French laboratories in 1971

C) African bees were brought to Brazil in 1956 for breeding but escaped

D) Bee stings were coated with a toxin, known as TTX, in South Africa in 1968

281

How do they kill their victims?

A) One sting is all that's needed

B) They only attack victims in water and hover above so the victim can't come up for air

C) They swarm all over the victim repeatedly stinging every part of the body for as long as a whole day

D) They cover the nose and mouth, suffocating the victim

Approximately how many people have been killed by 'killer bees'?

- **A)** 2500
- **B)** 1000
- **C)** 200
- **D)** 5000

In 326 B.C. who defeated King Poros of Punjab by hacking at his elephants causing them to trample Poros' own soldiers?

- **A)** Hannibal
- **B)** Julius Caesar
- **C)** Alexander the Great
- **D)** Attila the Hun

How many swimmers were killed by sea wasps in the 20th century?

- **A)** 6
- **B)** 38
- **C)** 65
- **D)** 102

Which creature is responsible for killing the most people every year?

- **A)** Mosquito
- **B)** Bee
- **C)** Shark
- **D)** Wasp

286

Which brightly-colored frog holds enough poison to kill 1000 people?

- **A)** Red-eyed tree frog
- **B)** Common frog
- **C)** Golden poison arrow frog
- **D)** Bullfrog

287

Which substance in a bee sting is harmful to humans?

- **A)** Gelatin
- **B)** Melittin
- **C)** Skelattin
- **D)** Tetrodotoxin

288

Pufferfish are eaten as a delicacy with most of their poisonous parts removed but they still cause a reaction in the person eating. What kind of reaction?

- **A)** A runny nose
- **B)** Burning throat
- **C)** Tingling lips and tongue
- **D)** Itchy eyes

289

How many people are trampled to death by elephants every year?

- **A)** 200-250
- **B)** 150-200
- **C)** 100-150
- **D)** 50-100

Us and Them

290 What are the effects of a bite from a blue-ringed octopus?

    A) Numbness and muscular weakness
    B) Breathing difficulties and hallucinations
    C) Vomiting
    D) All of the above

291 In Russia in 1875 how many people were allegedly victims of wolves?

    A) 161
    B) 122
    C) 63
    D) 208

292 What is Kevin Budden famous for?

    A) Eating a whole pufferfish and surviving
    B) Surviving 36 hours in the desert after being bitten by a snake
    C) Being the first person to be cured of rabies
    D) Sacrificing his life to capture a taipan snake and thus enabling an antivenin to be discovered

293 In the past 65 years, how many people have been killed by Komodo dragons?

    A) 0
    B) 12
    C) 32
    D) 65

294

The Choco Indians in Columbia use poisonous frog venom for what purpose?

- **A)** To tip their blowgun darts
- **B)** Medicine
- **C)** To tip their spears
- **D)** They give it to their spouses as an intent to divorce

295

What is the Palolo festival?

- **A)** A Masai tribe initiation rite when teenage boys go on a lion hunt
- **B)** A yearly snake hunt in Haiti
- **C)** An Alaskan bear-trappers convention
- **D)** A twice-yearly celebration in the Fiji Islands when the poisonous annelid sea worm surfaces

296

There was a famous rattlesnake hunter who used to pick up rattlesnakes by the tail and crack them like whips so powerfully their heads would break off. How did he eventually die?

- **A)** Old age
- **B)** He tripped over a rattlesnake in the desert and it bit him
- **C)** He picked up the wrong end of a rattlesnake and it bit him
- **D)** A living, severed head from a rattlesnake bit him fatally on the thigh

Us and Them

Freshwater stingrays have been known to penetrate wood and people's rubber boots but how long is the pain and recovery time if you get stung?

297

- **A)** 10 days, 5 months
- **B)** 6 days, 2 weeks
- **C)** 1 hour, 1 day
- **D)** 14 days, 1 year

Stonefish have been known to pierce shoes but what human muscles are affected, if stung?

298

- **A)** Breathing muscles causing asphyxiation
- **B)** Eye muscles causing blindness
- **C)** Masseter (jaw muscles) causing lockjaw
- **D)** Leg muscles causing paralysis

In 1935 a man was stung on the palm of his hand by a cone shell. What were the after-effects?

299

- **A)** The flesh rotted within 20 minutes
- **B)** His hand swelled up and had to be amputated
- **C)** There was a rash on his hand for four years
- **D)** Paralysis and death 5 hours later

What are dinoflagellates?

300

- **A)** Bloodsucking leeches
- **B)** Organisms in marine animals that cause anyone eating the animal to be poisoned
- **C)** Parasites carried by houseflies
- **D)** Venomous skin secretions on frogs

301 An incident occurred in a scientist's lab when a chicken and a dog died after coming in contact with a pair of discarded rubber gloves. What had been handled by the gloves?

A) King cobra venom

B) A phyllobates terribilis (frog)

C) The teeth of a Komodo dragon

D) Mosquito blood

302 In Africa barefoot farmers and huntsmen get bitten by saw-scaled vipers but die because they discover too late for the antivenom to work. Why?

A) They are usually too far away from a hospital

B) They look exactly like non-venomous snakes

C) They disguise themselves as branches so the men believe they are stepping on sharp twigs

D) The bite is painless and there are no external signs

303 The internal effects of venom from a saw-scaled viper take 12 days to develop. What are they?

A) It clots the blood

B) It enlarges the heart, making it burst

C) It breaks down blood vessel walls causing internal bleeding

D) It paralyses the muscles causing asphyxiation

Us and Them

What is the main cause of road accidents in Australia?

A) Kangaroos jumping in the road

B) Drivers spotting huntsman spiders in their car

C) Drivers being bitten by snakes hiding under their seats

D) Sheep wandering in the road

304

What dance was supposed to be prompted by a tarantula bite enabling the victim to flush the toxin from their body

A) Tarantino

B) Tarantella

C) Tarata

D) St Vitus dance

305

Intrigued by the myth of the tarantula and wanting to discover if people really did dance when bitten what did Oliver Goldsmith do in 1795?

A) Arranged for his servant to be bitten and saw that the bite caused itching and discoloration round the wound

B) Arranged to be bitten and found that the bite only caused mild itching

C) Dissected a tarantula and gave the venom to his dog

D) Traveled round Southern Italy until he saw one of the inhabitants bitten

306

307 **H**ow many people are bitten each year by redbacks?
- **A)** About 100
- **B)** About 200
- **C)** About 300
- **D)** About 400

308 **I**n 1983, one hospital treated 1136 bites from which spider?
- **A)** Brown widow
- **B)** Chilean rose
- **C)** Huntsman
- **D)** Brazilian wandering

309 **W**hat are the main effects of a sting from a Portuguese man o'war?
- **A)** Mild rash
- **B)** Round pustules
- **C)** Stinging and welt lines
- **D)** Major bruising

310 **C**ows drool an awful lot and make how much more saliva than humans?
- **A)** 10 times more
- **B)** 50 times more
- **C)** 100 times more
- **D)** 200 times more

Us and Them

In Indonesia, what animal do they make wine from?

   A) Snakes

   B) Spiders

   C) Frogs

   D) Termites

Which animals are used by police to find dead bodies in swamps and lakes?

   A) Snapping turtles

   B) Dogs (Golden retrievers)

   C) Monitor lizards

   D) Frigate birds

What animal, in Florida, is it legal to throw from a car?

   A) A dead hedgehog

   B) A live chicken

   C) A dog

   D) A spider

314 Which predators camouflage themselves in the water to look like floating logs?

- **A)** Barracudas
- **B)** Crocodiles
- **C)** Sharks
- **D)** Rhinos

315 How do poison-arrow frogs acquire much of their poison?

- **A)** By living in polluted waters
- **B)** By eating poisonous plants
- **C)** By eating poisonous insects
- **D)** Parasites

316 The skin of a rough-skinned newt is so toxic that it has no predators bar one. This one predator can eat the newt but loses muscle control for a few hours afterward. What is this predator?

- **A)** Hawk owl
- **B)** Garter snake
- **C)** Mongoose
- **D)** Cane Toad

317 Cane toad's skin secretions are so poisonous that any animal eating one will die within how long?

- **A)** 1 minute
- **B)** 10 seconds
- **C)** 15 minutes
- **D)** 1 hour

When are wasps most aggressive?

A) When they are eating
B) When they have just eaten
C) During their breeding period
D) When you pull their wings off

318

The poison from some toads has been used in what?

A) Rat poison
B) Antibiotics
C) Penicillin
D) Weedkiller

319

What continent has more venomous animals than any other?

A) South America
B) Asia
C) Africa
D) Australia

320

Which of the following animals can live for several days if its head is cut off but subsequently dies of starvation?

A) Cockroach
B) Fire ant
C) Goana
D) Flour mite

321